CALL IT PERPETUAL

The Poetry of

DAVID MICHAEL BELCZYK

Published by
Culturatti Ink
www.CulturattiInk.com

Inquiries should be emailed to: Orders@CulturattiInk.com

ISBN: 0-9712383-9-1
LCCN: 2006920009

First Printing 2010

Printed in the United States of America

Cover design by Ryan Alvis.

culturatti ink SM
A FUNKY LITTLE PUBLISHING HOUSE

To my friends

Note on the cover photo:

Taken at the Indiana Dunes, on the Southern shore of Lake Michigan, one of the most biologically diverse locations in America

Note to the Reader:

The poetry in this book, and everything I write, is intended to be read aloud.

— The Author

Please

If I become lost in the labyrinth of myself
Will you please pull me out
Will you direct me
To the heart of your hungry nation
If I come under the fire of my own senses
Or fail to control my speech
Or speak nonsense
Will you cherish me in my birthright
Worthy upon worthy in hallowed human halls
If I realize I am not my talent
Or my rank flesh
Please comfort my only natural fear
And nonetheless
I will create for you
And hope
For the beautiful smallness of my creation
What have we done
To deserve long talks of nothing
That end only with sleep.

DANCE

The plaza crowd
Frayed the gyrating circle
Of halfnaked bodies
The modern eyes engorged
Upon the ancient spectacle
Like the crumbs encircling
A finished plate
They close their circuitous mouth
Over the purveyors of sacrifice

The crowd thick
Scabbed with sun
Populates the haunted bodies
Whirling
Jaunting together and apart
Rattling their gold shackles
Upon their chests
Long pointed feathers
Spread a fearsome palm
Swaddling the temple heads
Of the cyclone bodies
A radiant earthheart halo plucked
The fingers bend supple
In the air thick with incense
And shouting

A line of saliva
Breaks from the mouth of a man
Who joined his ancestors without a costume
Whirling wearing jeans and suspenders
The mane of his long back hair
Summons the feathers

In the center
The splinter of a drum
Shivers the inflamed flesh dancing
Fortune limbers its gaunt frame
Expressing muscle
In the taught strings
Of its narrow shoulders pounding
The drum aches for him
Virulent it turns up its pale bruised belly
The rhythm of its demands
Is the pumping child masticated
It is the reason
His sinews gather thin and vivid

Around the plaza
Tall buildings
Raise their dead stoic faces
Toward the sky
Another stratum of abstraction
Created endurent in their paralysis
They are the cavern of the sacrifice
The whale's belly
For shipwrecked chronimity
The leach
That outdiscovers its progenitors
The unanticipated lecher
In beguiling horoscope

Surging loudly
The ancient design of the crowd
Cries Barabbas
Gawking awestruck at its own incarnation
Pierced by the splinter beating
It is the heart upon the plate.

Wallflower

Back and forth
Rock me to sleep
Like the breeze in the blanket of myrtle
Where I lie
Sweetly swallowing me
Coax along the bitter leaves
Down among their roots
Rocking in the earth
With the birth pangs of Armageddon
Cradling its cooing dependent baby

I watched you
At night
In blindness dancing
With a hitch in your step
Rocking and turning slowly
Back and forth
Across the multitude
Until you eased your face
Gently in a breeze toward distant me
I learned your eyes were jelly

Your wilderness churning
Winding
You plunged toward the rearing ledge
Six insurmountable inches

Back straightened
Arms thrust into the air
Waiving helplessly
Reaching for anything

I watched you
In the damp afternoon
From my perch in the pondering myrtle
Enter the rose garden alone
Like a madonna
Intricately you began to dance
In intimate worship
Swirling like an upset compass

You did not know
I was elevated beyond the slight stone ledge
Of the terrace
Very still
As I watched you collapse

You made yourself
Into an intentional tiny ball
Like a shut eye
Arms tight around your knees
I straightened
And reached
When I thought you had fallen

I only watched
You rocking
Rocking
Rocking.

TRAIN

The rumbling distance
Baits arrival
The subterranean cathedral abating
Honeycomb catacomb
Steal rails pour the nectar
From the black excised mouth
Illuminates a tongue of light
Dirt and oily air exhale
Predestined city manifest
The steam is on

Tunneled rock
Presides above the cold lake waters
We enter and execrate
Shrieking and exit
Commingled in the voluptuous
Unsuspecting the consecration below
Where timeless dead
Fade into the deep braided blue
Jujus of salvation trailing
Blessed consumed where I stand an eon after
In the mystery of another's god
Rumbling the train defies me

As I wait deific at the end of its tunnel
Louder and louder
It surpasses the anticipation of its climax
Consummation
Then headlights rocket past me
Silt whips my face
As the wind creeps eerily under my jacket
As the dead sink below the cold waters
As I pass out of the tunnel.

Pushing a Cart

He cannot speak
His cleanshaven waxen face
Is deeply furrowed
Slowly advancing the glum aisle of the train

He fools with the rowdy children
Pretending to hit them with plump balloons
He has tied
Or he makes their hair stand
With static electricity
His expressive face contracts then expands
Disappearing its wrinkles
The children do not know

To the parents
He mouths the prices
Of the things the children want

He listens to the parade of melodies
He will never create
An extortion of grotesque fraud
He will never emit
The voices sound the money
Bucolic
Among them his silent play seems gentlemanly
Even the trapping of divine

He is too old
But eyes the blond girl anyway
With weepy silt veiling her patient vision
She the sweetness of
His slow acetic bow dissolving
His paleness fizzes hidden
In her downcast eyes

The train is an arrow into the mute dilation
It has one vector
Rabid with optimism.

Aisle

The conductor bustles past me
Pressing toward the rear of the car

But he travels forward
Because of the speed of the train

His nametag is taut across
The sea of his muscular chest

Whadareyoulookinat
We have the same name
I said.

August

With this city
I am finished
I have seen beneath its diadem
When the early breeze
Lifted the dress of its smog
I have used it up
Before I ceased building it
So I call my incomplete
"Finished"
And claim the unhung and unhinged
The blank and blind stones
Are the intended font of joint creation
My part being finished.

WATCH

We passed beneath the collapsed arch
Where we used to enamor sheltered
It opened and we escaped despite ourselves

Now at the foot of the ancient cathedral beyond
We are astute beneath an equally old willow
Weeping
On a donated bench
In memoriam

She passed her fingers
Again and again
Over the round face of my watch
Alternately smudging and polishing the glass

Pondering the endlove
The love of ending
Cut to pieces
With the swirling of the second hand

I endure your seasons
Your root through and through me
Stone upon stone
But never higher than we imitate

You said
I wish I had bought you that new watch
For your birthday.

Quietus

We are alone in the room
Once alive with the parade of night
Now all the voices
All the music
Gone

We are clinging to the servant secret
That sweetened with evening
Before it learned the indiscriminate dawn
The overmastered hope
That dies with brightening day

Across the room
Beneath the glow
I lay my hand upon
A pocket watch
With a mangled face

Sad among her buttons and needles
And thread
Halfburied
Beneath the horizon of her mending
Gathered in a decrepit cardboard box

My celibate
Deliberate fingers
Turn over its soft muted silver
Smooth as skin beneath
A century of tarnish

Curious the aching pleasure of function
Winds the knob
Startled to hear the watch tick
Startled by the enormity of the sound
In the hard room

Wearing her knitted cap
And coat already
Take it
She swears to me admitting
Only I don't know how to set it

Starving for the secret
I pry at the shell of the watch
Force against its clinging past
Peeling open the alarmed innards of the moment
Its gears whir

But I cannot intercept them
The fragile pieces campaign the spring or break
And some longdeparted hand
With wiser precision than my own
Has slid the tiny lever toward fast

I seal the disgust
Of knowing its anatomy
And pry at the cracked bezel
To interfere the hands directly
But it will not depart the body

It clings mightily
Protecting the only knowledge of the mechanism
Her hand falls upon my ambitious hands
Maybe that's how they broke it
She says

We conspire with
Speechless enwombed
In the inevitable pageant of the sound
Happy for a moment
To be enthralled by the problem of our demise

Maybe
I say
You have to wait until
It is the time on the face
And wind it then

I set the watch upon her desk
My dumb fingers gently orient it
Right angles
To the rough
Approximate corners

Slowly I feel its cracks shards
As I draw away
And away
And away

I imagine her returning to the quiet room
Alone and hearing only the watch
Its human eloquence empties me

The spring of its brash heart winds and unwinds
Drumming

It is loyal.

Mode

The peace of my age in pieces
I lie upon the grinning hours
Sharptongued handmaids of the past
Side by side
Share my secrets
Like I cannot hear them
Flashing skill to compare the smoothly fetished
End product of my days
Expression flitters around their filigree athletics
Like an ant over my foot
Makes me heave to conjugate the circumstance
There is enough of me
For their hunger
If I retire humbly to my secrets
But selfish cultivation ekes out my flavor
Anxious about the feast
Were I thin and tough
I would be alms.

Dinner

I have mistaken me
Latent too late
And pining obvious
In the now surrounding
Voice rounding down
Erosion sounding in round
The permanency of a long
Withering click in the lock
Talk me softly easing
Moaning the keyed jingle
A tumbler melody
A somber tone that
Bears its teeth promiscuously
Play for me
I am on the platter
Just beyond the click
Just beyond the honor of the tune
Worming around in the
Stomach of the stony labyrinth.

Beneath the Rotunda

They are there
Behind the iconoclastic
Ignorant by will
The growling shrinking void eclipses
Casts a shadow in
The belly of the architecture republic
Where they fold in squalor

The cities convulse with need
In the twilight arrogance
Of participle progress
Breathtaking spasm desires
Endurance partible
Meted
While one soul in its communion
Empties with
Every empty soul
They are there

A tour through this body
Show me
No expense was spared
In the construction
It cries pangs of need
Constructed well enough to teach need

No expense spared in its construction
The sovereign body
Opulent to deny need
Freedom from want
Its children
Learn its hard lessons instead

Accidentally discovered
Down the stairs from the glistening dome
Beneath the rotunda
They are there
In the chamber circular
Hiding amongst thick stone pillars
Sleeping
Talking
Playing cards
Anything but eating

The room has the stench of sickness
The gaunt specter reality
Hunts about
Looking to eat alive

So shut up the mouth
Whose speech could admit them
Close the hands
That fear they will honor them
Close the eyes
That might learn
Why the red of the flag
Borders their pure white

Turn back up the stairs now
Of your own will
Or be turned out with the rest of us
At close
Into the deathly cold

We are there
Too thirsty to salivate
At our other selves
Spoilt by our very existence
Hunger numbs with the body
But the sovereign body
Hungry for soul
Wails through every season.

Mansions and Cathedrals

The bitter comfort
Memory
How long I toddle
In a world of faith and wealth
A wealth of faiths
Entrance the dusty corners of my being
Slough of hair and skin
Swept away from frequency
My body and blood
The frayed tassels along the hallway
Throw

I spin in my tiny corner as I
Heave my eyes toward the towering height
Immense to admit me assumed
In a gorgeous embrace
Insistently greater than
The cold draft wilting
From the soaring stone upon my bare back

My smallness makes me subject
Encircled
Roiling the phantom heights
Into shafts of colored light
Cutting candle smoke
Into scattered apostolic dust
Swept by body heat into the shadows

I locked in my marvel
At the high moulding
At the polished shafts of light
The babbling rich rooms
Where gossiping servants
Clean and clean and clean every corner

I found a treasure in my home
And buried it in
The blind spots of the acanthine pillars
When I awoke in the afternoon
Afraid to be alone

The calamity of chagrin commissioned
Numbs me to pain
Like I slip naked into
The autumn forest's clear icy pools

I count up all my dust in my corner
Every speck of a pulse
Sickening pressure dwindling
Youth spent in always
Gazing at the beautiful handiwork
Alive within the homeless fame that
Dies to dwell in me.

Meat

I
From my birth
I became
The lonely
One of choice

Led by her
Wrinkled frame
Gracious age
To the block

I the hope
Progeny
Ignorant
Work of knives

Butcher scent
Bloody nose
Discover
The back door

Narrow hall
I press close
The flayed deer
On the hook

Labial
The spread ribs
Forced nature
For my dream

Network red
Veins tissue
Muscle slit
Power rent

In my face
Flies tracing
Fresh salt lines
Killing line

II
At the gate
Bright rancor
Stifling heat
Industry

Too old now
For fearing
Commanded
Spread remnant

Where aching
Bodies past
To repeat
The knifes' work

Still like blood
And salt the
Decayed breath
In my nose

All of it
Eaten fast
Good eating
No hunting

Enter slow
Christmas Day
Heavy gate
The canal

Charging head
First into
The Godlike
Production

III
Old enough
To fear again
Hunched shoulders
Slow shamble

I approach
The destroyed
Red comrade
Motionless

Bled and puffed
Infected
Animal
Death wasted

No salt smell
No fresh tang
Blue putrid
Odor stings

Crippling
Calloused hand
Reaches from
My belly

Life remains
Unmended
Already
Through the gate

It was me
On the hook
From my youth
The hunted.

Shard in the Hand of the Maker

Symbiotic stained glass
The shelter of our union
The flower of your face relegated
To the course colored chips
I am the image cast upon the floor
Only a crude blurred echo of the design
Created by your restraint
The resonance of perpetuity
Lingering confident(ial)
In the house of an ancestor

Your volume startles me
Anathema to my dyed darkness
A looming delicate hand to smash
Its languid frame untelling of its strength
Looming until the strike
Strike against the stained glass
Please please

Shatter it and I will be lost
All my color
Even my crude replication
As you pour through the glass making me
My blurred memory of design
Erased by your flood
Of indistinguishable brightness

Because of this shatter
Then I will simply be the shards of glass
Remaining on the floor
Once my filter my frame my forever
Now I am my shattered creator
I will bear your frame
Your pall
I will carry you.

Toast to the Destructor

In the glass
I am transfixed
Its apocalyptic shawl
The smiling glaze
Upon the colorless cavern of purpose
The instrument in my hand
Swallowing intent fast
My glutton to plumb the empty well
Me hollow glutton
To shatter more elegantly
More intimately
Fulfilled by my filling
Its sharp accomplishment draws blood

On my lips
Praise to devotion
Poured out in courage
What I siphon in fear
When I faltered at the hinge momentum
And devotion
Brought together the two shapes
And made them
Shards
Spilled out in tumbling fragments
The poisoned well
The erupted glaze

On my lips
Praise of sylphic passion
Poured out love
From the lithe taste
Drained transparent
I loosed my salvo
Raised my cry
Cresting alone in night
When I flung the vessel
Empty well
Against the blind wall
Good for servant echoes

The glitter
Awed the clouded light of the alley
And I ran
Afraid to inhale
My cutting discontent
Spilled over the table
With the color of a punctuation mark
And I ran
Afraid of the shame.

Nimble

Moonlight unveils the tree Goliath long
Stretching its web of black
To the seditious mud
That must touch to believe
The gentle figure knows what it is not

In the dazzling glow
It is a black petal stippling upon the earth
Its weightless whisper stealing
It does not sink

The mud is ravenous
To be painted black the image
Boasting that it swallows all things but elegance

Adoration craves thread the tissue inseparable
Gazing at its other self disembodied

Twisting in the dark agile heat

The tree recollects a source to quench
Precipitate upon the ground leaping

An image for what it hides buried
And has not seen
It is because of its secret

The tree grows from its shadow
Nourished by the void it carves
Made by the consequence it casts
Hoping its roots quiver as it quivers
            as the black quivers

A reversal of fortune
Reflected at the fulcrum of the flack loam
It looks not at its secret
But to its likeness
And makes its strength to bud.

Palm Sunday

I come out of the sleep
Of infinite extinctions
To fill myself to annihilation
To make the nothing created
To come into glory
To loathe void
I am formed you unexpectedly
Radiant you from my tragic heart
Overexuberant now vellumthin

I open wide my body
To embrace all distance that could separate
I burn in testament
Purging by flame the test
To pour out a deafening expression of you
Rending myself in the streets
To bawl my tender aching soul
That hurts me in the places you make it free

But what could I say that is worthy
My life is a levy decaying
New torrent surging against aging form
I will spill
But I am denied knowing what I contain
I wait for the unbalancing rains of spring
Germinating
Hoping an unrealized hope
To be produced inherent and inevitable
From nature itself

I am our child that hopes to be conceived
Love from void
Life from nothingness
When you become my proclamation
I cannot say anything worthy
But will relinquish myself into worthiness
Pushing my tears into your eyes
We do not have to exist
And would not know the difference

There is nothing I
Nothing we
Nothing all
In forever of creation
Nothing equals the splendor of love
I cannot speak
Cannot cull
Cannot create
Anything anything irreducible
Everything from me and of me dies
Save I love and give all myself

And you
Who are you
Because you are clashing and flawed
As I am attentive to your disobedience
Only love of the imperfect is perfect

I will not sleep
Though it is already tomorrow
If I sleep
Today will be yesterday
I want it forever to be today.

Shroud of a Mane

So the answer then is no

I am a sire shade
The protectorate of my regal mane
Squeezing into complicit mousehole compline
Into the little house of my meal
And running along
The cramped space within the walls
In search of crumbs

I pushed valiantly
To opine the whole of my mane
Through this tiny crack
And now a crumb is all the sweet
In my desert
The justice of my kingdom
I let it stick delectably to my tongue
It is too small to melt in my mouth

But I am patient
The creature abiding its kingship
The king abides in its creature
The morsel of my kingship
I am the scraps I ferret out
Lifting them up
With the light patting of my rough tongue
Can you not hear me scuttling

My answer then is no
I cannot govern from this compromised position.

Zoo

The lion paces the bars
Its slack haunches shifting
Paws beating retracted ferocity
The hungry tooth roots in the tender gum
The ravaging claw nestles snug in the soft pads
Its metered steps
Swallow the tether of anemic chronology

Behind the bars
I ponder in my animal
Behind the bars
The lion is not patient

Dividing in the tabernacle of
My mimicking mitosis
My mind breeds the pacing
Breeds the plots of the bars

O my animal
Safe to study in its receding retention
Convicted in contention
My corporeal works
Make its concession condemned

But the lion stands forth
Upon the perverse lock of its penury
To exhume the debtors' gaol in fancy parody
Bland and studious folly
While I admire very much
Foresight and the strength of my bars
The precious pound of flesh
That holds the beast
But not its slightest murmur

The lion rolls the gravel in its throat
Unfurling a dry rough tongue
From a dark cavern
Choking on the purring immensity of the sound
It expectorates the expectant
Throaty spark of maturation
A division of selves
Staring out through the bars of the cell

The toothy gap
Widens a yawn unto its breaking point of
        production
To grovel becomes the growl
Upbuilding
Shrieking
Like the broken spine of the apian way

Terrible in its volume
Hacking again and again
In the repetitive climax of conquest

Behind the bars
A pale hand grips my forearm
Beneath my coat responsive muscles
Flex and tingle.

Edified Captive

Those immobile eyes know
The meekness of my victory assuaged
Frozen in my raw receiving
Given me naked endurance
That I am incapable to preserve

Back away
Back back you insatiable gratitude
You too much disquiet me
Beaming your incredulous gaze

I will yes
Will have yes

The flood of birth
The master scribe of my flesh
And my back
Now the supine and craven writing desk
Scribbles scribbles
The callow curve of my spine

Those immovable eyes see my cursive
The gossip of my breathing breathing
They lie bare before me
My eyes discourse the darling curl
Darting between the momentary sojourn.

MEIOSES

Give me the new myth of your name
I do not seek
The transgression of ancient forms
Gray haze of indecipherable migrating
I nominate all
Entitle all
Choose all
Emanate unrequited nature in its halflife
Without place to be enshrined
Billowing up to brilliance
Without companion
Without transmittance

Stupefied with a fearful
***** how did they *****
Nursing a missing explosion of brilliance
All is incremental
Growing like blood vessels spreading
The body too incremental
True in its tiny progress
One by one by one by two by four
Thickening scars

See me growing
Billowing up to brilliance
You are flush
Stood too fast and blood cannot
Rusty it is suckled
Sapped by the sweeping
Train of your dress
Progress wedded dressing.

Lunar Eclipse

I draw my passion
From the failure of nature
Ennobled by the gleam of
Nature's eye entranced
Its shimmer a reflection
Not my source
Burning off the vapors of nobility
The silver orb
Draws out the wailing dog itching my rhyme
Bids dust know sublime
Frozen in the hope of the solstice

The silver portent
The shimmer of a parched and bitter dream
Dancing cycle
Pregnant and mysterious with the seasons
Outmoded only by my larger shadow
Me interposing
A sickened nature fasting
Born of love
The bastard couplet
Of the triptic dance
Orbits to extinguish
Its enamored

I am the silver
Once dust now ennobled
Err I reflect
The intelligent illegitimate of the triune
I am as I am made full
Or as I am sharpened and fasting
Poured silver from the taproot of life
And howling back irreverently
Steal my love
Hush in the overspilling blackness
Bare now the heat I bore

The shadow is receding.

Solar eclipse

Me intertriune
Interother now
Enter knowing
Me interposing
Engorged on the errant love
Of passion's apathy
I lap the flames of my ennobler
From their disembodiment
I craft my superstitious majesty
In our covenant
I am coveted
Transmuted from my frailty
To shame the blue eye blinking

The gaunt face I draw to me
Grows full suckling
And robs me of my splendor that draws me
The golden genesis of our dance
Now is the cause of its creation
Holds me enraptured to you
Cycling between cool elegance
And the burn of your ravishing
Each the extant victim aligned
I will your superposition
I exonerate you exulted

I learned the dull red of your hiding
The blush of prayer mixed with betrayal
When you ebbed
When you summed from darkness
Your brilliant tangent flare
Silhouette of light
Fragile ring flashing
When the shadowmaking mother
Lauded our souls into blinding forms
But now it is your bloodmoney silver
Casts the shadow
My circle cradles your mysterious womb
Your vanity in my steady being mercy
You siren
Now see the face of your love blackened

The shadow is receding.

Ochre

My maladroit interdiction
Shimmers progeny on my palms
Upfacing I make the table splint
Bear it on the deeddoers with a stiffstraight back
Strong enough to bear your pulchritude
My palms cracked from repeating deeds
The deeds from repetition doing
On its own sad inquisitive volition
I am interdict
Bare you on this raw plank
Later I will heave at the splinters in my palms
Sore to touch the fleshy deed
Against the splendor fabric of a name
Working the linens roughly beneath the running
A lighter shade of ochre seeps the incursion.

WORKERS

We slipped behind
The impressive fault of fabrication
On an evening cold with daring
And stoic blame
Stovefaced like iron
Against the heaving hot
Mob of the fault
Bundling up the awe of their
Ascending vision
They surged and were repelled
From sensation judgment
In the vernacular of segregation
Behind the lines
We raised ourselves
Upon the dyptic charisma
Sublime before the
Autonomous
Aeons accepting
And watched the lower class
Applauding.

Handprint II

A handprint on my table
Cataloguing life's ecstasy
Seared visual it endures
Until touch will destroy the touch
It endures
If I with
Hold my hand
That was its maker

I have not the power
To create or destroy
I cannot break my might to submission
I do not own it

I am naught beyond my earned rights
When I think of your body
Arching taut its taught power
In the palms of my hands
Bowing poised and terrible
Brisk and fetal
Pouring like steam through my fingers
Tendrils like
The tight moist tendons of your back
Against the wood
Against the table

I was afraid
And left my print
When I reached out
For something steady but unreal

I am not worthy of this gift
I am infinite in finite print
Within me
You do not deign to give me
Give me back
Press the image
I choose it

You demand it
That I should receive
What is greater than I can know
Receive or die
And so
I will not deprecate what you recreate
My humility will not be ingratitude
Or refusal

Because you choose me
I will devour you
My eyes will consume you
Unblinking
I will smile the teeth of your liberty
From the gullet of my choice
I will press out your fingered testament
Your elegance
Framed by my hands
Unintended altruism systole
Self conception.

And I Think

Who owns this clever scar
A rich surface signed in the reckless past
Not anticipating value
Racing jealousy to the sharpened point
Eyes down

My hand sweeps the flaw
In the smoothed antique table
Coalescing the brim of ugly things I want
Having chased away the meager
Might of purchase
So many things I want to claim
By touch
The touch of self
Foolish over my tactile self

And the hordes it could convince
And the dandy pride it could horde
A lightest touch
Again and again forms the score
That smiles condescendingly
Then insists it does not mean so

I incise
My pink gums taste the fear that sharpens me
That I might lack trinkets to lose
One day I feel so young
The next so old
Looking to what has past
Alternately
To what can be owned
To call mine
The individuality of these beaten treasures
Showing their marks
That I am not the first

Burn widening scar
To acquire the perfect seismic blight
Of imagined history
A fine piece
Truly
A finest piece
And I think
Someday.

Warm Hands

Against the pale curtain
Closed on our enclosing
The frigid slenderness
Found each their five ways
Into the hollow of my warmth
The white tuft of my palm
Against the cold work of the white
Chilling brilliance manifest in gift

The kind siphon knows the way of my pulse
Its tooth in my heart
Which smiles the shard to know it is given
Possess me
In the stream of life you divert
That I make life from lifeless
Energy
Shame me in my fire by your need
I forgive any loss that brings equality

My sum burst free the division of its bank
Torrents from presence to lack
I will that I should drain
Drain and bleed in my infusing will
Entreating the white flesh to ebullient red
To thrive within my sheath
And constrict without

Residing in the perfected skin
A plume deliberate
Within the subsuming shiver of love
I will go again into
Inviting the same frigid pain
A wanting captive
Captivating the entranced cabal
I clutch
Even total dissolution
For the sweetness of the play
I will give until all is equal
Then sleep in the folds of the nowwarm.

PEARL

You only
You only know
My latent buzzard cry
My swollen famished cry
Embryonic and gnashing teeth
Against my human pearllike struggle
The beauty wrought from struggle
Arrogant beauty
Swirling gossamer vanity
You had to be
You had to be my beauty
And now only you know
My sullen buzzard cry
My scavenging cry
Buzzing upon your burning ember ears
Boiling up my cry
My genuflecting cry
I am all picked clean
Down to this pearl skeleton.

Accoutrement

The black veil petal
Tongues my opening name pried
Unfolds the path to your jaws
Like the damp fertile tongue
Of the black earth
Extended
To the frontispiece horizon

You are the mantle
The folds in which I hide
The lips entreat

Open on the pearl
Cabal

I see the original sin
At the core of the creamy white
Its capillaries
In me concentric

The polyp trees
Black on the horizon
Reaching from the soil caress
The round iridescent haze
Slumbers upon the fingers
The vessels in the nourishing lung
Encystation center in the coveting

Hidden roots
So fine
So extensive
They will not be removed without destruction

Bite your flaxen tongue
To see the origin
Close the crushing jaws
Marvelous brute
Annihilate the pure spectrum of the white
A fine powder in the mouth
Like I eat my own
Delicate ash imperfection
That spawns the pearl
Caution
Or the implanted mother
Will be lost among the sand

Parasite pearl
Encrusted with the honor of its genesis
Enamored with the shimmer
Behind the jaws
Before it goes down
Slow and large
The glyph of your throat
Like the parasite fiend within my cells
It dies with me
It struggles so the cell may live

Your elemental tongue
Is in my fooled mouth
From the kiss
My gift subfusc
The product of immeasurable aeons
From within me
But not me
I produce the nacre.

Habit

My world is slender
Day to day
Upbringing me a genteel sense of need
But slender is as its accoutrements
Crafted glamour clamoring
To slink along
Off put
In a tempting haughty gait
But for its show
Slender is tame
And welltamed
By thickwristed dishonesty
The thought canvassed from the meaty palm
Over pulpy
As it directs the delicate flame

Slender health is
Slender age
Needy and frail
Brittle pale
Sown up in ornament
Ornery like the meticulous wrappings
Of finicky eons
Bound daylong to the attractive need
The night brings sultry peace
Never so bony.

Corday

I did not expect a voice
Rather that you would be locked
Wearing the course and delicate necklace of
    your gift
The femininity of your insurrection
As my imprisoned scaffold tongue
To split like the raw red petals of my eyes
My raw little revolution bare and resting in a tub
A wry smile soaking through the tragedy
The malady of slender hands
Fine and idle
Tall and narrow
From the idle I expected voice
But not from the serenity of your handiwork
Seeing as you are before my eyes.

Migration

What love is pinned up now
Against the low clouds
Wriggling ash
All mossy brick and frightening gait
Beneath the low clouds
Pinned up now
Softspoken like the moss
Rippling over the brick consequent
In speechless consanguinity sequence
Strict and motionless lament
They hold tight joints
What love
Wears so well its fetters
Such unassuming peace
Strolls beneath its captive fringe
Lucid defeat hanging
Rains down
To put feet on the wet moss.

Speak

The still smooth surface
Untraveled unwept and unheralded
Until I harbored your language soft
Reflections of words unknown
What meaning do you shape
Within your deliberate shape
Gentle with my knowledge
You teach me the cause and consequence of
aesthetics
Veiled in moments unforeseen
You remain veiled in delicate smiles and glancing
Profiled brilliant against the loneliness of desire
You rest in small discontents
They prove the value of difficult communication
But in this reflection
Deep beneath the onlooking stars
That explain the Barcelona night
We are both wondering
At the distance captured
In the glowing curves of your mouth.

Behind the Bar

Sumptuous service you
Emote charity
Dispense the ancient trembling of belief
Supreme knowledge
That tempts the endless trains of faith
You shape patience with your patient shape
My patience to know
What I call supreme
The sparking of your backwards glance
At my helpless curiosity
Forgive me to amaze me
I have not trusted in the lovely
As I have believed you
Without words.

Married

I

Ceremony awaits its dour dowry
Vernal and nervous
Unwinding on the spindle of
The long aisle
Blushing like rose petals
Swept under the gown
Red powder tickling the lace

The procession blushes
Into union
As it kisses the vows
Sealing their joints
The white hardens slowly like wax

Trembling hands shimmer conscious
The new feeling of the rings
Expression is repeat after me

While pomp sweeps the turning heads
Unraveling row by row
The crowd purses in one focus
With corsages matching
The red lips of promise

II
The nervous crowd is paralyzed
Albicant as the frightened woman
Shrill cries are limber
Through the celebration
Silent hall
Pauses echo between her shrieks

Her father doctor holds her
Down tight on his diagnosis
But she is alone in her terror
Rumors of the cause
Dance about the crowd murmur
Embarrassed to look

They frame her body shuddering
The aperture of her heart open
Sealed
A photograph steals the bride
Flush over her shoulder
Afraid the joy will turn somber

The icy singular sound
Enters the bridegroom
Lonely primal paucity
Lopes out of the reception
They are all so sorry in syncopation
That they forget it left

III
I am sad and feel convicted
Suffering innocent infertility

I slide the garter
Further up the leg of my embarrassment
It loves how I caress.

THREAD

Adulteress
Make me your won
My impenetrable hour is divorced
Permeate me
Vapid pattern
You can escape after your cure within me
Less one stitch less none
The keystone
Of my triumph arching like a beggar's word
The fledgling
Prostrates
To your matchmaking pious only one
I was found
Nose down
In the boughs of the green green grass
My bearing fruit
The color that
Our hooded night (finding in parting) will not
Relinquish know you now
Precious only one
Could you flutter any faster your butterfly
Stitches.

Two

I - Vows to No One

I do not believe in circumstance

But you are a victim of circumstance

I will be a selfvictim
In the dregs of responsibility
In the quicksand of an agile heart
Anchored in the trace of your ravishing
When I was nothing in your subsuming eternity
Climbing toward our justice
Taking the steps two at a time
I am still damp with the perfection of your dream
Like I never expect to see you again
Like you are what they said
At the last marriage in history
I play out all my worth for you
In the blast of a dented old horn

No
You will be a place and a time
A garnered dream

Our joking prod
Knows me to spear me
I acquaint myself
By smearing across the laughter
Conjoining the blurred vision of humor
You are inappropriately kind
To my inapposite inside
Awfully soft on your smile
Lush pouring hot looks
Into the onlooking cavern
Of my enraptured solitude
I am nothing but a small crease in your smile
As you spin exhibiting your foreignness
I flex over your winking superstition
I am come like expulsion from paradise
I make up
I finish
Craving you my madonna
Indulging a glance down the continent of your veil
I will walk
Lending my knucklebiting fate
To a shameless self destruction
I would collapse into only your arms
That would grant shameless resignation

I have you know
What you would steal
In the selfish night

I am pursed persuasion
Snapped shut
Our purloined lewd inquest
Lipped over pay
Words over speech
Overworth
I am not capable of making heroes

I will freeze in the second you are emboldened
And race the candy shell
Concealing my engorged river
I channeled to you in all those lonely hours
I will collapse the shell
Impatient for your love
And drown cold in your scalding profile
Nose to nose
Succumbing the drawl of your touch
Your warm preoccupations
Tumid in your aspiration
I empty for your warm breath
You are lurid fantasy

You open my eyes and I say
There is no one there

You are a victor
Not a victim
Accept that we are fools
Before the fate of our divide
And do not hurt me
Please

I will cover the earth
In the fire diamonds of your name
I roar creation for you
Poison my mind with you
The mind that you love and cannot be replaced
I will give everything
Even my spirit to the poor in
Rapacious
Wrap us needless
In toothy life's unreserved laughter
I would love you
Would love you
Would serve you
Would beg for your provision
And be redeemed by my despair

You would love me like I am free
          and make me so
I would be precious to you
Cherishing the indelible eternal memory
Of your song to me
And our unequalled voices

I am the distance from you
Not that between us
You cannot fold me
As you do this time and place
Circumstance loves you
It will leave you fulfilled
And looking impressively vulnerable

I can be obedient like a child
Believing like a child
Joyful in devotion
Against the world's pouting
We could play and play
Across the scar of history
Hovering just before the trumpet blast
Of guilty creation
I swear I am
I swear I am in you

I profess you in all circumstance

You do not believe in circumstance

I do not believe in circumstance
I do not believe in ceremony
I do not believe in circumstance

You are a victim of circumstance.

II - Colloquy

I hang upon a promise
Hush promise before your genesis
And do not protest my weight
Or the constructs of your making
I have agonized over your beauty
Never to see your august face
How will you feel
When not only you
But the act of you
I have accomplished
I am accomplished
Through the supernal body
I touch the undertow of creation's awe
Foreshadow to forehead and of one mind

Face to faces
Share my breath
I enshrine me another sentient being
Engendered intellect commingled
Ascending love of prematernal primacy
Believe me
I inhale
Your exhale
Let me touch your temple
Embrace me in the body
The protokronos
The protognosis
It is my inseparable
Inseparable now from you are
We are clasping a void
A one of two
A one of the one
A void raised to love's concurrency
On our credo.

New

We were though two
Made all the world's restless children
Arched sanctimoniously
In the bitter potency of flesh realized
Like long and limber spires building
Consolation of our frail sketch figure
Climbing dizzying altitude
The melting candles of finite thought
Dipped wick the staircase of the curved spine

And kept climbing
To the tip of the sacred
On regal height the parched eye
Blinks blinks
But has lost its tears

We are preserved in the graymartyred halflight
Presiding over the stern slur of a replica
All was the haze of arête
The potentate
Beneath the magnificent basking modality
Discursive strength in the tone of one
    gray eternity
Course by course
Hardened melt
We absolve in the resolute diffusion
Glory adopts a shroud that it may be perceived

I am singularity
Neoteric lightskinned for her imperial grayness
Kneeling like Phineus
Obfuscate my newness
All the sky appears as radiant slate.

Yes

You would wouldn't you
Set me up center
Of the escarpment
The flutter of your scarf
And your hair my scapular
Flecked with frozen white

You would wouldn't you
Step lightlike step halfwise
Scuttling up the scrap
In the halflight flutter of your eyes
You would wouldn't you
Over now the monarch pouring
Alleyway shadows our fluttering
Barking scribbles
Upon the escapement whirring

You would wouldn't you
Have me fluttering with your hair
With your curls
Looking over
White cliffs to white foam
To write home
To write poems

You would wouldn't you
As I am peering over
To see the base of these cliffs' miraculous
Shiver
Push me
Over your escarpment
And I will be one puff of your air
That you may not splendor away.

Alibi

I was the
Awesome snarl of your armies
Their spoil
Angry at the conqueror
I was the
Strict obedience
To your tearful order pleading
Deliver the pale graven phalanx
Glowering bitter like rank citrus

I was the
Idol carver for needy believers
Without belief
Gulping down the azure distance
To fuel the charge of my evercreation
I was the
Squelched beauty in the eyes
Hiding behind the shouldertoshoulders
Dreaming love to know
Why the brute broke ranks

I was the
Flung down forgotten doll
Filled with another's stuffing
The child played with me
And tore me open
I was the
Anticipation of the crescent
My fingers smeared pale blue
From the powder of the hydrangeas

I was bound up
By a command having always been issued
Is issued
Will forever have been issued
Masquerading the eternal now
Before the purity of the seasons
I was on this barren rock of desire
Racing through a vacuous sore
I was the abandoner.

River I

I injected myself into the current
Pushing against my hips

Carried away in tendrils
I am drawn out among the rush

Enter the womb of the current
Embracing the surprise of your clamoring island
Your shivering dare

The river embracing me
I am current in its heaving

That we should have this eternal summer
This eternal bloom
Eternal fruit
Reposing in the womb of your tiny house

Please do not leave

Before we were nothing
After we are nothing
We are here in the current
Where I slip through your hands and away.

River II

I possessed the pure snow
Of your sleeping skin
The frozen tongues baptized us
Who I willed to crush
Like white petals to powder
That I would bathe in the perfume figments
And accept nothing
So I need give nothing
Until

Our communion froze over you
Over your secret wound
Gush beneath spindles of frost that
Lull over in the tether of your pain
Caught in eddies
They dissolve to nothing

I push
Unlock the coursing sable of the husk
To where you are bleak white
Entering the heavy depth
To spring my own
Cold sweat
And kiss the soft blush of ice
Like age that seems before its time

While venerating
I am swallowed

Rolling my lips
To the vow of silence
To clutch
Cold stripping my flesh
Or drown in the current

I could not breathe
Only wrench free my cry
Into
The inevitable smiling somberly
The volume of my fading lips
Proof of my weakness
When my all
Is no more than an echo
From the forest of shadows
No more than a whisper
To the roar of grief
Its transparent fingers
Thin and closing my numb words

But I did not drown
I followed
To where you were pouring out
Gushing the wound
The life blood
Life cycle
Blood without violence
Blooming to creation
Identity upon me
The red red red
Fierce like the desire to live
It will not brook reduction

I finding it was you pouring into my mouth
Not my breath
I am hunger for the boon of your exhale
It was your flesh at my lips

That which I swallow

I feed upon your surrender
Where I mistook the world
Because I am the burn of friction
And you the letting.

Pier I

The hard human clay of your cracked hands
Touches my unraveling beatitude
Let me steady your trembling
Short walk for proof
That forgets its nascent glory
Uplifted on the shimmering blue

Distant pumping factories
Stand beautiful in the icy slanted light
Let me hold tight the harbors
Of your shaking hands

Your lips quiver
My soul shivering as I enfold you
And lose my place
Shuffled around amid the pain of choice
That shames the clean pain of loss

Did we light up all that shimmering in Eden

I dream blinded
As the sun radiates behind your shadowed face
Our hair flying at the wisp of the edge
Like we were never here
Like we never wanted to leave
We left.

Pier II

I

Heavy air depleted breath
Thick with bugs pelting me like rain
As I soared through the stillness

Through the dark sweet smell
Of grass and lavender
Toward the lighthouse

Down the right side
Past the rusty poles that
Form the spine of the pier

The water extended endless
Into the black pristine
Obscure syrup slithering a cloak of fog

Its thrilling still immensity
Lapped me against the edge of terror
That I should be swallowed by its vacuum

As though I never existed

II

I sped away
On the left side of the rusty spine
A bug lodged in my squinting tearing eye

It squirmed suffocating
At the edge
Of my pupil

The still black rimmed with red
My sight would not swallow it
My tears would not wash it free

Trapped and frantic
I felt it shuddering
Searching in my swollen pain

I did not stop
And soon the tumult turned stagnant
After I passed the beaches

Though I never felt the captive come free

III

You were there
I saw you
Just before I entered your shadow

A supine silhouette
On the hot concrete of the pier
The host on the abiding palette

One leg bent
As you stirred and groaned
Among shopping bags filled with trash

You startled me
Suddenly so close to your edge
I turned quickly

And I ran.

Waiting

When will you come
I feel my passive heart beats unsure
My chest is an open curio
The precious moving parts tick the living seconds
I am a grand experiment under glass
When you

I have waited all day
Hoping I might discover your curious secret
Watching
My polished cuirass
How long you are peering through
Without knowledge

Open on me
The ornate doors of my expectant breath
Their exquisite patterns
Carved of experiential waiting
Eye my fractions matured in wait

But the latch is delicate
Do not do penance in swiftness
Or I will not keep others out

What reward waits for me
I preserve
Only to lose the mystery of my experiment
When the glass will
Suddenly become offensive
When you will

It is my nature to wait
Created to hope or die
When
You are the beauty of nature's simplicity
But do not be its indifference
Better not to come
And save my wait from vanity
By crushing me
But
Come.

Self Coronation

The faces watch history
Unpleased and nonplussed
Not knowing it is their moment
They curse their inertia
They do not command it

I am the shimmer on this moment
To be dashed
Should it stir beneath the inquiring light
A terrified bauble
What if I am mishandled
While they applaud

I reach for the proud slip of logic
To ground me the obsolete crown
Its plodding will trod me roots of proof
I want it
Give it me
I am reaching

The arcane pages dispose of the moment
The disgrace of justice that
To be equal must be blind
They lend empty words
I am afraid of my value.

Succession

Supplicate me
My retinue and my vainglory
With sinister arms draping fiat
Supplant my courage
I have courage
But the fear to displace it

Why sculpt me
When I could instead be dumb
Like a sheep before the shearers

Or perhaps disgust me just enough

Or simply do not be where I wait
Like a large bough of flowers hung to dry
And forgotten
A vague sense of longing self
Feverish denying its own fate
In the lust of oppressing and obscene giving
The unenviable power to choose the world
Draining its body out of its own splendor

Or be instead a tiniest love
The little power of an insistent crown
That inspires its own loss
Or expects me to be awed
Because the crown conquers
Crawling back
Into the garish gape of its yawn

But I will not
Even the loveliest head

God
Breeding
Just
Shows

In pursuit of ancestry's tattered visage
I loom larger than the way I jut my chin
Amidst the fateful clouds
After all
The fashion of anticipation
The adhesion of receipt
Perhaps
After all

Just disappoint me

Shall I have the gall to cry pity.

Creep

Slowly
Just turn light the gravel of the walk
No sound heavy enough to draw an echo
Creep darkly
Express no brightness
No ornamentation
Creep silently
Not sharing gracious right to utter
Make deliberate pronouncement
Soft tread by each

Do not
Wake
Conscript a little place in peace
Bejewel it only the lumination of necessity
Make a good need
Eat it up
Squelch the fire
And fast

Now sleep
As the gracious of the still sleeping
Who did not find you an intruder
Come morning hollow
With a niche and a plot
Take a deep breath
Where is this daylight.

Dream

Tell me your dream young slave
The master gives you permission to speak

In my dream
I die
Afterwards there is nothing
I realize my vain maturation
Just at the mature cusp of conscience
My memory parish dissipates
I forget as I know I am forgotten
I cease
I am forced to know it
And I wake gulping for air
Like I have been holding my breath
Like God holds my head beneath the water
I vomit my heart
Slamming in my ribs like it may rend
And I am lonely

Tell me your dream young slave
The master gives you permission to speak

In my dream
I die
Still I continue to exist
I know myself extending
Formless and endless
Forced to know timorous eternity
And infinity
They are enormous and will not engage me
I wake up gagging
Swallowing air
My guts twisted
Slick with putrid sweat and burning
And I am lonely

So you are the willing slave
The helpless wrath
The segregated seed and womb
Alone without its strictures
The cooperation
That exceeds the selfobedient one
Sharing our reconstituted break

You have infinite permission to speak
Provided you do not.

Homecoming

No love is so pristine as hope's agony
No heart so perfect as hopes the shunt of pain
Oozing blithe between
The scalded fingers of compassion
Love evaporates in the coddling hands
Eddying round the tender brand
But will not compose

My eloquent toast
That fain hope is pride hope is grim
To lick its grinning chops
At me
Teeth so sharp
They lacerate the tongue

In dire search
Love's challenge tends to soss
And intention denigrates in the draft
Hope becomes currency
Spending all self for its glory
Smithing the image
Burning for what selfless might resolve

And then the tyrant fear
That hope should be anything but
Its glimmering outline
Controlled
Dying for a peaked lonely ghost
When it would bound into a heart
At the command of devotion
Whom is commanded

We can boast eternal
In this empty room of fear
And alternate hope
And eternally go with flowers to the grave of
our love
The petals like vague intimacy
Accomplished through
The intermingling.

Dead Tree in a Café

My young eye
Rolls homage and euphoria
Tangent
My sharp profile
Makes a crescent of the blue iris
Peering from fresh skin
Like unspent obedience
To my right

The loose bark
Puffed and fragile
Naked
Its withered fingers
Stretching toward the hazy lamp fixture
Its flagging zenith
Affects the oncesupple stalks woven below
Before tightening the knit

I examine it slyly
Like a beautiful woman
Who pretends to be unaware
And fools me
I rap the table
Rattle my saucer
Another poem
Another cup.

Culturatti Ink and David Michael Belczyk are pleased to donate a portion of the proceeds from this collection of poetry to Culturatti Kids.

Culturatti Kids is a national non-profit organization that works to inspire young writers and advance literary arts education. For more information, visit www.CulturattiKids.net.

www.ingramcontent.com/pod-product-compliance
Lightning Source LLC
Chambersburg PA
CBHW051449290426
44109CB00016B/1686
* 9 7 8 0 9 7 1 2 3 8 3 9 8 *